# A MIRROR TO MY LIFE

*Genevieve*

This is the noblewoman Genevieve, riding through the night all alone in search of her lost lover.

*Australian Wild Flowers*

# A Mirror to My Life

## PERLE HESSING

# HENRY HOLT AND COMPANY

## NEW YORK

First published in the United States in 1988 by
Henry Holt and Company, Inc., 115 West 18th Street,
New York, New York 10011

Library of Congress Catalog Card No: 87-21272

Edited by Jill Hollis
Designed and photographed by Ian Cameron
Produced by Cameron Books,
2a Roman Way, London N7 8XG


ISBN 0-8050-0712-1
First American Edition
Printed in West Germany
10  9  8  7  6  5  4  3  2  1


ISBN 0-8050-0712-1


Cameron Books is grateful to the following individuals and
galleries for providing transparences: Dr Harry M. Bloch,
Sophie and Leslie Caplan, Leonard Hessing, Max Fourny,
Dr Frank S. Lucas, J. Lockhart Nelson, Professor R.G. Wake,
Galerie Eisenmann and Galerie Neumühle.

The quotation from *Under Milk Wood* by Dylan Thomas is
Copyright 1954 in the United States of America by the Trustees
for the Copyrights of the late Dylan Thomas  by whose
kind permission it appears in this book.

To my husband Siegfried for helping me to achieve my aim, and to our son Leonard whose
encouragement gave me the confidence to go on painting.


I am grateful to Jill Hollis for her help with the text.

# PICTURES

## COLLECTIONS

The majority of the paintings reproduced in this book are drawn from private collections in Britain and Australia, but the following are owned by galleries:
*Mary's Vision after the Crucifixion*, Musée de l'Ile de France, Vicq, France; *Cheder*, Galeria Contini, Caracas, Venezuela; *Golem 2, Golem 3, Cain and Abel, Job and his Friends* and *Balaam's Wonder Ass*, Galerie Eisenmann, Böblingen, Germany; *Genevieve* and *Peacefully Together*, Galerie Neumühle, Schlangenbad/Wiesbaden, Germany; *Moses Triptych 1*, Musée Laval, France; *Vision of a Gas Chamber* and *Tereczin*, Yad Vashem (Holocaust Museum), Jerusalem.

# INTRODUCTION

I was born in 1908 in Zaleszczyki, a small provincial town in Galicia on the border with the Bukovina and at that time part of the Austro-Hungarian Empire. Here my father, Leo Hirsch, was born, like generations of his family before him.

I lived in Zaleszczyki only until I was six, but I still have vivid memories of this lovely little town and the countryside around it. I remember orange-coloured rocks, green and golden trees, and the river Dniester with its soft yellow shores and water so clear that you could easily see the pebbles on the bottom.

Most of the houses in the town were just one storey high. The busy marketplace always fascinated me: it seemed full of stories and dreams, especially when it carried on after dark.

And there was a feeling of history about the place: on the town hall was a cupola with a statue of a Turkish soldier holding a spear, dating from the days when this part of Europe was over-run by the Turks.

My father was a printer and bookbinder with his own workshop. I remember, from a very early age, being shown all manner of beautiful books that came into his hands for rebinding. Father made sure that we attended school and then took it upon himself to add to what we learned there. Every Saturday afternoon, when the workshop was closed, he would gather us round the big workbench and tell us stories: folk tales, old Hasidic legends like the Golem or Mystical Wedding on the Graveyard, but above all, stories from the Bible. Quite soon, my brothers and sister grew bored with life at home and wanted nothing better than to escape to the excitements outside. As I grew older and became the only one still at home, my father went on to discuss more serious and complicated parts of the Bible with me, as well as telling me about things of interest that were happening in the outside world. He had the urge to share his knowledge and I was a good listener. I think I always had a vague sense that I would be able to draw on elements in many of the stories I heard and use them to meet challenges. But at that stage I had no clear idea of what they would give me. Later I discovered a similar sharing experience with my husband, Siegfried, through our reading the Bible together, and so I have been able to build on the knowledge that I gained from my father. Reading the stories now brings my home back to me more surely than anything else.

I have now painted my interpretation of most of the stories I knew best, sometimes with the legends that have grown out of them. Often one particular aspect, a person or a relationship, has fascinated me, and so I have emphasised or developed that in the painting.

My first taste of being alone and really seeing things is fresh in my memory to this day. At that time, parents were very careful to shield their little girls from life: you couldn't go out alone, there were things you shouldn't go near – you certainly shouldn't touch animals. Nevertheless, my curiosity normally got the better of me. The feeling of being free in nature was to become very important to me, and I grew up loving animals.

One beautiful spring night, my mother and father decided to go for a stroll through the town after they had finished work. I was about two-and-a-half or three, the youngest child of the family, and as my brothers and sisters had all gone out, my parents put me to bed and left me, as they thought, safely at home. My bed was next to a window that faced towards the market square, and the noise and movement outside stopped me from settling. It was very early spring, not even Easter yet, but so warm that half the town was out promenading. Outside, a street lamp shone brightly and prettily in the fresh, warm air. As soon as my parents had gone, I got out of bed and let myself out of the house. Nothing was locked – you didn't need to worry about that sort of thing. Once in the street, I saw crowds of people, all walking about as if it were daytime, and I sat down on the pavement beneath the street lamp. Above my head I could hear a buzzing noise, like a strange sort of music. I looked up and saw a sparkling, glinting sight like a never-ending firework, a magic array of blues, reds, purples and greens, more intense than any colours I had seen before. It was a cloud of insects with iridescent wings. When one of the creatures scorched its wings and dropped to the ground, its colours vanished; that made me terribly sad.

As I was sitting there, my parents arrived back, gathered me up and put me back to bed, more interested in my safety and a good night's sleep than these enchanting wonders. Once I was in bed the magic sight outside came back to me again and again: the dark sky glittering with stars and then, under the lamp, the extraordinary luminous colours of the *Maikäfer* (cockchafers). Since then, I have seen a lot of paintings and a lot of colour, but never anything to match that intensity.

When I was about four years old, my grandmother on my mother's side came to visit us. She brought for me a wonderful china doll, far more beautiful than any I had seen in Zaleszczyki. When you pressed a button, she could say Ma and Pa. I was so thrilled, I thought she was a living thing and loved her very much. One day, my brothers started teasing me, saying that it was not a good doll and they would break it. So I went and told my father. Nothing happened, but I decided to hide the doll under my parents' bed whenever my brothers were coming back from school. One day, my younger brother said that the time had come to break it. The older boy laughed, and before I could do anything, the doll was broken. How broken I was – just like the doll. I kissed every little piece of her, but it was no good. I thought I would be upset for ever. My mother saw how I was in despair and said, 'Don't worry, I will buy you a doll that will never break, that nobody can harm.' And she bought me a little timber doll, which I grew to love greatly and kept for many years. It was a lovely wooden *Mulattenkind*, a mixture of brown and white. But I never forgot the wonderful creature with the golden hair that I loved so much, and as soon as I started to paint, the experience came back to me; the timber doll was the subject of my first painting.

Another experience might seem banal to an adult, but felt like an enormous injustice at the time. Childhood suffering is perhaps the greatest suffering and can happen just because adults don't take children seriously. Later, this memory helped me to realise how important it is always to keep your word with a child.

When I first started going to school, I wanted a new dress. My mother said that of course I must have one. So I looked forward to this treat. When it came to my first day at school, my mother put me into a frock that was a mile too long and a mile too wide. I asked her 'What is that?' and she said, 'This is a beautiful frock, it is your sister's nicest frock. We will get it altered for you and it will be just right.'

At the time my older sister seemed like a princess to me – I was six and she was eighteen. So I accepted this dress with all the pleats to make it fit. I went through the first class, through the second, and then there was a celebration at school. I asked my mother whether I could now have a new dress. 'Oh yes,' she said, 'Of course.' And the same thing happened. I had been taught to be polite when I was given something, so I swallowed my disappointment and went to the party in a cast-off. But although I kept quiet and behaved myself, I thought it was very unfair. There is a wonderful expression in German *'abgelegte Herrschaftskleiden'* – what high society throws away. That is what I had to put up with.

Next time I asked my mother for a new dress, she bought me a beautiful new black bow to put in my hair. I was a bit suspicious, but I was still promised the frock, and her smile reassured me that this time she really meant it. July, August went by. The end of the year came and still no dress.

My father was a cultured, gentle man, full of patience and ready to listen when things went wrong for me. So when the disappointment became too bitter I went to him and tearfully complained that although I had been promised a new frock lots of times, I never got it. And I asked him whether I was allowed to say that my mother had told a lie. 'God forbid!' replied my father. But I insisted that my story was true and that I was not exaggerating. Then my father embraced me and said, 'Perle, next year I will see to it myself that you have a new frock.'

The next year came, as it surely would, but instead of a new frock it brought with it the First World War.

In the summer of 1914, my father was called up. When I saw him in the grey uniform of the Austrian army, I scarcely recognised him. My brother also went off as a patriot. Zaleszczyki was very near the border and quite soon we were threatened by the Russian advance.

All the men had gone to war, but it was clear that the rest of us had to leave in a hurry. Some people from my aunt's farm came and picked us up in a big wagon with four horses. When everybody and everything had eventually been loaded on the wagon and the children were perched on top, we set off across the large steel bridge over the river Dniester, into the Bukovina. We had hardly got to the other side when the bridge was blown up to stop the Russians crossing the river. The whole cart, complete with luggage and children, was lifted in the air with the force of the explosion. For adults, our escape must have marked the beginning of a huge up-heaval. But small children have little awareness of this kind of danger – I found all the fuss very exciting. We went from place to place in the Bukovina, staying with relatives, until finally we came to Czernowitz, my mother's home town. She declared there and then that she would never leave it again, no matter whether it ever became possible to return to Zaleszczyki. Could she have had a subconscious premonition that much later the destiny of those who remained in the little town would be carefully planned extermination?

My father, who had been at the Russian front, returned from the war an invalid, very badly injured in one leg. Slowly he began to think about what he should do next. He was sorry not to be going back to his home town, but this time he had to give in to my mother. There were still a lot of Hirsch relatives in Zaleszczyki, which by that time was a part of Poland, and after he had recovered a bit, he went back to sell the few things that remained. Our house had been burnt to the ground, but he still owned the plot of land on which it had stood. So he sold the land and was paid in Polish marks, so many banknotes that he had to carry them back to Czernowitz in a little suitcase. But when he went to the bank with this money that was going to enable him to establish a new home and make a fresh start, the bank clerk said, 'You would be better off using this to paper your kitchen walls than bringing it here – it isn't worth a penny.' That was a terrible blow for my parents. They had literally to start from scratch. But my mother was a brave, sensible woman and she applied herself to the long, slow task of rebuilding a home. My brother, who got back from the war a year later because he was imprisoned in Italy until 1919, helped my parents to start again. My sister was by this time grown up, engaged, nearly married. Slowly my father began to do some hand-binding, but he never had a business on the scale he had had before.

When I was sixteen I met and fell in love with a student in philosophy. This young man aimed not to collect titles and awards for his studies but to treat his involvement in philosophy as a life-long challenge and mission. My mother was not very happy that someone so young should have fallen in love, but we shared with my father an attraction to mysticism and the study of bygone ideas and times and we spent many happy hours in discussion with him.

In 1926 I married the man I loved. But a shadow was soon to pass over our happiness with the death of my father. Perhaps he had a sense that his life was drawing to an end. Certainly he had always said that he would return to his home town to die, and suddenly he wanted to go back to Zaleszczyki. My mother had tried to dissuade him from making the journey, but he was set on it. Eight days later, on a Friday morning, he died. His sister had gone into his room earlier and had seen him praying – he was a very devout man, not orthodox, but traditional and conscientious. When she came back with his breakfast, he was deep, deep asleep, still at his prayers. He was buried in the plot that had been set aside for him, next to his parents in the town he had loved so dearly: his final wish had been fulfilled.

My father had not been able to wait for the arrival of a newcomer to the family – my son was born in 1931 and named after his grandfather. Soon I took my infant son back to my birthplace. I saw that the little town was as beautiful as I had remembered. It was midsummer and the little boy played just as I had on the golden beach and in the clear water of the Dniester. It was the first time I had been back since 1914.

Between 1926 and 1939 I lived the more-or-less routine life of a housewife in Czernowitz. When Germany invaded Poland, a trickle of refugees began to appear from across the Polish border, our first sight of what was to become the destiny of so many people living in that part of Europe.

From the beginning of the Second World War, Czernowitz was occupied either by the Russians or by the Germans. What happened, especially to the Jews, in Eastern Europe was incomparable in scale and horror with anything history had witnessed before it. The way I have decided to deal with what happened is to leave things to rest and get covered over by time. Others have already talked convincingly enough about these things and described them much better than I can. I have no desire to reopen historical scars and make them bleed again.

In 1945, after life under Hitler and Stalin, we went to Bucharest to join a ship for Israel. The ship sailed, but in the Dardanelles we were picked up by the British and given a choice of being sent back to Rumania or going to yet another camp, this time in Cyprus. They didn't want us to go to Israel yet, because there was already trouble between the Arabs and the Jews. So for eighteen months we looked through barbed wire at the land where Aphrodite had been worshipped. Sometimes it was so cold and wet in our tents that we couldn't get warm, sometimes so hot that we couldn't breathe.

Finally the United Nations declared Israel a state and at last we arrived there. But we soon realised that we could not stay. This new country, struggling to establish itself, needed strong young people to do hard, physical work, and we were just too weak and worn out. We had survived since 1939, and we simply couldn't do any more work of that kind. We decided that we had to go somewhere else where life would be a little easier. And there was our son Leonard. Throughout all the trials, he had had teachers and studied, and so he had to do something. We didn't want his talent to go to waste. When he had the opportunity of being accepted as a pupil of Fernand Léger, we all lived in Paris for a short time, until Leonard transferred from Paris to Sydney University to study architecture. We decided to move to Australia.

The first five years were difficult. Like many others, we had to start from nothing in a strange country with a strange language. The Australians have a saying, 'He who cannot settle here within five years had better look elsewhere for an easy heaven!' Times were not too rosy for us to start with, but we worked hard and managed to get established.

After about ten years, by which time Leonard had finished his education and achieved a good reputation as a painter, my health, which had not been strong since the war, began to demand its rights. My husband and son said, 'It is time for you to have a holiday, after working so hard.' My eyes were very bad because of anaemia. I already had a cataract. Other things, like arthritis, that were a result of the war didn't help. So Siegfried and Leonard decided that I should take a whole year and go to Europe for a complete rest and a thorough medical check-up. I sailed with good friends, who had had the same sort of experiences as us. The first stop was Italy, so that I could see Venice and Rome. Then I continued on my own to Vienna, where I went to look for any relatives who had survived the Holocaust and to consult doctors. I found Gustav Hessing, a cousin of my husband, now a recognised Expressionist painter and Professor at the Academy of Arts in Vienna, and discovered that my husband was listed in the Austrian History of Literature. In Australia I had been advised to have an eye operation, but I consulted a Viennese eye specialist for a second opinion. Doctors in Vienna were often especially careful with people who had been through the things we had endured. 'If I knew when your eyes would have to be operated on,' said the Viennese doctor, 'I would be a prophet. What you need is to relax and improve your general health, and then you will find that your vision will get better.' I was also advised to try to leave the past alone and live for the future. So I rested and took a treatment and, on Gustav's advice, began to explore all that Vienna had to offer: the opera, the theatre, the museums, but especially the art galleries. My health improved enormously. I looked and felt well for the first time in many years. I particularly enjoyed the work of the traditional painters, the Old Masters. I liked the Dutch paintings, interiors with people going about their business, and I loved the work of Rembrandt. He painted the subjects he liked: he couldn't care less if it was a Turk or a Jew or an African. I like his objectivity and honesty. Gradually, as I looked at more and more pictures, a feeling began to surface from deep down that made me wonder whether I might ever be able to do something like this. It reminded me that even when I was at my weakest, having just come through the war, I had a kind of belief that the fact that I had survived meant that there was something in store for me, some challenge to live for. Perhaps this was what I could do. I had no idea how to go about it, and decided my ambition should remain a secret, but before I left Vienna I did just hint to Gustav what was in my mind. Gustav responded in a spirit I shall never forget, telling me that I should be true to what was within me, that you should never suppress the kind of feeling that comes from your inner being. I went on to Israel to spend a short time with what little family I still had and returned home to Australia with a feeling of optimism and challenge that did more to rejuvenate me and heal the sicknesses of the past than anything a wise man of medicine could offer.

Once home, I started to think about painting. But how do you start? I had no knowledge and no experience and had learned no technique. But one day I just decided to try and so while Leonard was out, I went into his studio and used a bit of paint, a bit of chalk and mixed them to paint a picture of a little girl with a timber doll, from one of my childhood memories. Then I thought, if Leonard sees this, I will not tell him who did it, and if he thinks it is all right, then I can consider going on.

I put the drawing on his door where he would be bound to see it as he came in. 'Who did this lovely painting?' he asked, 'Why do you want to know who did it?' I replied, and he said, 'No, who did it?' 'Well, as you think it is so lovely, your mother did it' said I, and he was delighted. That gave me the confidence to go on. Soon I wanted to learn something about the techniques that real painters use. Leonard told me that I should just go on as I had started. 'I wish', he said, 'that I could unlearn some of what I have learned.' But I insisted, and he finally took me to see Desiderius Orban, a great Hungarian painter who had founded an art school in Sydney, and said, 'I bring my mother to you as she brought me many years ago to Fernand Léger to be accepted as his pupil.' Orban turned to me and said, 'You are of advanced age suddenly to want to start learning how to paint. Have you anything to show me?' When Orban had looked at the paintings I had brought, he refused to teach me on the grounds that schooling would take away the character of my work. So I started to paint at home.

People reacted differently to my paintings. Some joked that I had inherited the talent from my son; some had a hard prejudice against naives, only liking properly trained painters; but some, to my delight, loved the paintings. During my first year of painting, I had a colossal boost when three of my paintings were selected from the six hundred submissions for the Blake Society's annual exhibition of biblical paintings in Sydney.

I spent eighteen months working non-stop, pouring all my energy into this new challenge and at last forgetting the hardship of the past. I had decided that all that sickness should be put out and left behind. My first solo show was opened by Desiderius Orban, by then over eighty years old.

After I had been painting for some years, I was asked to go and exhibit in Germany. I didn't go the first year they asked me, but I was sent an announcement of a special anniversary at the same gallery a year later, and it seemed to be a kind of indirect invitation. It cost me a lot, but I decided that it was time to go. I believe that hate doesn't lead to success or help civilisation. I wanted to show this and said to myself that this would be the first proof of my decision to abandon the past and start afresh. I would go there and face the people. And I did go and realised that they too were trying. Seeing this was a great thing for me.

In 1977, I went to Amsterdam where my husband was attending a commemoration of the tricentenary of Baruch de Spinoza's death. My husband was offering his third homage to Spinoza and I contributed a picture to accompany this. My appreciation of Spinoza dates back to the feeling of closeness I experienced with that young student who so willingly shared his youth and his philosophy with me and acted as an ambassador for Spinoza's teachings. Being in places where Spinoza had lived and thought impressed itself upon me greatly. Perhaps the reason why I felt I could begin to translate some of the philosophy into pictures was that I shared some of his sources of inspiration: biblical themes, legends, parables, folklore, the Cabbala and mysticism. It was a great challenge, not one I would ever have imagined for myself, but my husband said that Spinoza holds a kind of magic which can inspire an echo in writers and poets, so why not in a naive painter? So I painted *Scenes from Spinoza's Life*, including all the main events, his ambitions and even his dreams.

In 1982 we were invited to a Spinoza congress at Urbino in Italy for the 350th anniversary of his birth. My husband submitted a paper on Heine and Spinoza and I tried another pictorial contribution, this time on a theme with which I could identify very closely, Spinoza's suffering connected with a historical event in August 1672 in the Hague.

A man called de Witt had been imprisoned after being wrongly accused by the mob of some misconduct. He was found not guilty by the court, which ordered him to be set free. But the mob were not satisfied with this expression of justice and stormed the prison so that they could march him along the streets and hang him. Spinoza, alarmed when the rioters came near his house, decided to put a notice on his door that read 'Ultimi Barbarorum' – last of the barbarians. Luckily his landlord warned Spinoza of the grave danger this put him in, and Spinoza wisely gave up the idea.

The things that I want to express very often come out of stories and ideas that my husband and I have shared. I suppose what has attracted me about so many of the ancient legends and stories is their quality of timeless revelation. Very old places like Jerusalem, Prague and Amsterdam sometimes hold this feeling too. In Prague, I visited ancient synagogues in search of traces of Rabbi Löw, creator of the Golem, and then painted my three episodes of the Golem story. Other influences have been the works of Rabbi Nachman of Bratislava and Isaac Bashevis Singer.

Knowing about these truths, these important observations about life, and wanting to express them has done much to help me avoid the trap of wailing about getting old. My painting has given me an escape from isolation and from the various trials and tribulations that could have got the better of me. There is an old Hasidic blessing: 'For the unlearned old age is winter. For the learned it is the season of harvest.'

Despite the advanced arthritis that cripples my hands and arms (and sometimes threatens to cripple my mind with the pain), I am assured that no sign of the pain or disability shows in my work. In fact, although I sometimes find it hard to hold the finest of my brushes, the experience of painting works like a wonder drug and can even make me forget the aches and pains I am so conscious of most of the time. I can become so absorbed that it feels as though there is nothing between me and the canvas; I have the impression that something is being drawn out of nothing. If, between paintings, I glance at my easel and there is no canvas on it, I experience an odd pang, maybe like a hungry man at a table with an empty plate on it. Often I have thought that the painting I am working on must be the last, and then I find that there are more and more last pictures to be done.

Painting seems to bring me a lasting alertness, a way of viewing life and continuing to learn, and also a means of liberation. Sometimes when I sit in front of the easel, it is as if I am discovering something from inside me that otherwise would never have emerged. When people ask: 'Do you still paint?', I feel as though I am being asked, 'Do you still live?'

Painting has helped cure or put to rest the harshnesses in my life, and I hope the naiveté in my pictures will help people who look at them to overcome obstacles in their own lives.

Perle Hessing
London, July 1987

Among the pictures in this book based on biblical subjects, some reflect the most widely recognised versions of these stories, while others incorporate lesser known interpretations or even legends that have grown out of them. For those who wish to follow up the biblical texts, the references (in order of the pictures' appearance in the book) are:

*Abraham's Sacrifice*   Genesis 22:1-18
*Abraham and Hagar*   Genesis 21:9-21
*Jacob's Dream*   Genesis 28:10-17
*Adam Naming the Animals*   Genesis 2:19-20
*The Seventh Day*   Genesis 1:31 and 2:2
*Expelled from Paradise*   Genesis 3:23-24

*Cain and Abel*   Genesis 4:8-15
*Joseph in Captivity*   Genesis 40:1-22
*Moses Triptychs 1 and 2*   Exodus
*Job and his Friends*   Job
*Balaam's Wonder Ass*   Numbers 22
*Judah and Tamar*   Genesis 38:6-27
*The Witch of Endor*   1 Samuel 28:7-25
*Merkaba*   Ezekiel 1:4-15
*Daniel's Vision*   Daniel 10:5-12
*Daniel in the Lions' Den*   Daniel 6
*Elijah and Elisha*   2 Kings 2:1-15
*Noah's Ark*   Genesis 6, 7 and 8
*King Solomon and the Queen of Sheba*   1 Kings 10:1-13
*David and Bathsheba*   2 Samuel 11:2-5 and 26-27

*The Village Fiddler*

## The Four Seasons

This picture shows the various stages that people's lives go through, just like the passing of the seasons: childhood, youth, maturity and old age. First there are children, then young lovers, then parents with a baby, tilling the soil, preparing for the future, while the old people sit quietly, having worked all their lives and earned their rest. The wheel in the centre symbolises how the same progression continues and continues.

## The Shtetl at Night

In Eastern Europe, *shtetl* is the name for a little town. Zaleszczyki is the *shtetl* where I was born, and this picture represents much of what I remember seeing as a very young child. Our house was in a street which looked on to the marketplace, and as far back as I can remember I was fascinated by this market. It was so bright and there was so much going on. My older brothers and sister were allowed to go out, but I was too young. I heard strange tales about some of the people there. The market traders used to talk about the headless ghost of a dead stall-holder who came back to haunt them, and there was the horrifying story of the poor young woman who had had an illegitimate baby and to mark her out, to show her shame, the people got hold of her one day and shaved her head. It always seemed to me that the dark alleyways and the shadows must have creatures living in them – they seemed so scary, but the thing that I found most frightening was an alley between high buildings. On top of one of the buildings was a statue made of dark iron of a Turk brandishing his spear, and I used to feel him towering above me, able to see everything that was going on.

## The Blacksmith

This shows one of my earliest memories in one of my first paintings. I was staying at my aunt's farm up in the hills, and one day the milkman let me ride with him on his cart. On the way round the district we stopped at the forge. I remember being very surprised that the thin little blacksmith dared to lift up the hoof of the huge horse.

*Mother Caring for Her Sick Child*

*Chat in a Narrow Street*

## Cheder

Cheder is like a sort of Sunday school, or even a nursery school for the tiny children. This is an old-fashioned room and the Hebrew teacher is not very rich: in one corner is his bed, in another his kitchen, in another the table where he sits with his young pupils and teaches them about the Bible and Hebrew texts. Cheder is the Hebrew word for this room that the teacher both lives and works in.

## Abraham's Sacrifice

Here is Abraham with his son Isaac after one and a half day's journey from their home to the sacrificial fire in the hills. His son does not suspect that anything is wrong, although he did notice when they arrived at the place that the usual sacrificial ram was not there. One of the servants gathers wood to build up the fire. God has demanded of Abraham that he sacrifice the thing which is most precious to him, his son. But God never really intended that the boy should die. He was just trying to see how pious Abraham really was. As Abraham raised the knife to kill the one he loved most, an angel stayed his hand, saying, 'No, look behind you. There in the thicket is the ram you must sacrifice.'

# Abraham and Hagar

This picture took me a long time, both to paint and to work out before I started painting. I needed some way of keeping each part quite separate, while still having one lead on to another, and in the end I used a serpentine form with the events scattered along it. At the bottom right you can see the tent of Sarah and Hagar. When Abraham realised that his wife Sarah would be unable to bear children, he was sad, for he wanted an heir. She suggested that he take her Egyptian maid, Hagar, which he did, and presently Hagar had a son, called Ishmael. Even as a tiny child, the little boy played at fighting: he was later to become an expert bowman. In the Jewish tradition, age is treated with respect, but when Hagar saw Abraham's devotion to Ishmael, she felt that she was the more important. Sarah became more and more unhappy. Then one day three strangers arrived at Abraham's tent, and he offered them water to wash their feet, and food to refresh them. Soon one of them told Abraham that his wife Sarah would bear him an heir in a year's time. The couple laughed because Sarah had never been able to have children and she was now much too old, but they were assured that this really would happen. One year later, to her amazement, Sarah did have a baby, Isaac. When Abraham had a party to celebrate, Hagar and Ishmael laughed at Sarah and mocked her. Abraham was torn. He knew this had to stop but he was loth to throw out his son and the mother of his child. But God agreed that he should get rid of them. So Hagar and Ishmael were sent out into the hot, dry countryside to find their way back to Hagar's homelands with nothing but a flask of water and some bread.

Hagar walked on and on. She and her child grew hotter and thirstier as the days passed. At last Hagar became frightened that her child would not survive the journey. She left her little boy in the shade of a tree to rest, and wept. Then an angel appeared and said, 'Don't worry. Turn around and you will see a well,' and sure enough there was a well behind her. When they had drunk from it, Hagar and her son were able to set off again, and survived.

At first I was angry with Abraham for doing such a cruel thing: turning a young mother and her child out of his house. He was a rich man with many animals, many fields, many servants, and all he gave her was a jug of water and a bit of bread before he turned her out under the burning sun where she might easily die. But then I began to sympathise with poor Sarah who had done no harm and was constantly humiliated by lucky Hagar. In a way, both of the women were trapped: Sarah by humiliation and anger, and Hagar by her own jealousy. She couldn't bear the idea that Abraham still loved his first wife. This is why I put in the two lambs, to symbolise the innocence of the two women. Human beings are basically innocent but they still do things that hurt each other and trap themselves in situations that do great harm both to other people and to themselves.

## Jacob's Dream

Jacob was on a long journey. Darkness began to fall, and he found a place along the road to spend the night. He used a stone as a pillow and soon fell asleep. Then he dreamt that he saw a ladder reaching up to heaven with angels on it, walking up and down, and he heard a voice saying that he would receive rich land, and his family and descendants would prosper. When Jacob woke up, he realised that God had been all around him, and that this was a holy place. He then took the stone he had rested his head on and set it up as a sacred pillar.

## Animals at Dawn

When I was very young I spent summer holidays with my aunt, deep in the countryside, and I have misty memories of seeing deer jumping about in the woods near where she lived.

# Peacefully Together

A fantasy. This is how life could be . . . but isn't.

## Heimweh – Longing for Home

Here is a young shepherd boy who has been working far away from his family, whom he has missed desperately. Now he is weary from his long journey back but thankful to be nearly home.

## Jobless Weavers

A picture of unemployment, and of the sadness and poverty of idle hands. The couple live in this one room and have hardly anything to eat. Over by the wall the loom, neatly hung with pattern samples, is idle; the pincushion doll is discarded and the sewing machine has nothing to sew.

*The Family Outing*

## Abandoned Woman in a Winter Landscape

I don't know exactly why this woman is homeless. She might have been thrown out of her home with her four children; she might have left because she couldn't stand it there any longer.

## The Golem Cycle

Rabbi Löw lived in the ghetto in Prague in the sixteenth century. He was not only a holy man but also clever in science and astronomy – a very learned man. The rabbi saw the results of the overcrowding in the ghetto: everything became dirty very easily and unhealthy and he wondered what he could do to help. Then he realised that he should try to keep the place clean so that no sickness would occur, and he had the idea of creating a robot which he called Golem to do the work. This Golem was made of clay. When it was constructed Rabbi Löw thought, this Golem is big and strong but now I need to make it move. And the vision came to him that he should put into the open mouth of the Golem a small scroll of paper on which were written three holy words. This done, he commanded the Golem to shut his mouth.

The Golem obeyed and the rabbi decided to test out his creation further. He ordered the Golem to clean the synagogue, to clean between the houses and to keep watch over the boundaries of the ghetto to make sure that no harm came to its inhabitants. The Golem became invaluable in the work it did, but would only obey the voice of the rabbi. One day Rabbi Löw ordered the

Golem to bring water to the ghetto, and then in the afternoon went to pray and meditate. He became so deeply engrossed in his meditation that he did not notice how late it was getting. All this time the Golem had gone on fetching water. The people became frightened because no-one but the rabbi could stop it – and they were terrified that the ghetto would be inundated. Finally someone found the rabbi, still deep in his prayers, and told him what was happening. He quickly saw that there was a real danger and told the Golem to stop. But the Golem had been in motion for so long that it just went on and on. The rabbi was distraught. He decided that the only way to stop the Golem was to destroy him.

The third painting sums up the whole story. In the top corner is a picture of the Golem in the place where it is shut up by the rabbi every night. All around is an impression of the cramped life of the ghetto. That is what being in a ghetto is like. It means restriction of your life. You are not a free person. Because there is so little room, much of everyday life happens in a higgledy piggledy way outside in the street. There is a bootmaker, a secondhand shop, even a coffin being carried by mourners, chickens running around, the synagogue with the bucket of water outside for cleansing. In the middle you can see the desperate people praying that the rabbi would be able to stop the Golem flooding the town. In the foreground is the Golem, broken to pieces by the rabbi who is sad that such a useful creation ended like this.

## Mystical Wedding on the Graveyard

Long ago there was a terrible sickness in Europe. A wise man, a rabbi, who was watching the people around him die like flies, pronounced that the only way to stop the plague, to lift the curse, was for a young couple to have a wedding ceremony among the graves of the victims. If they defied contamination and death in this way, they would defeat the awful disease. And this picture shows the young couple who agreed to do it. The mother is grieving because she is sure that her son will die, but the candles show that in this macabre place there is a reason for celebration. The light in the sky dispelling the darkness is the sign that the couple will triumph.

## Adam Naming the Animals

Eve is playing around, frivolous as ever, with the snake with whom she has such an intimate relationship. The angels are there because there is a story which says that originally the angels were supposed to name the animals. When they tried to, though, they didn't know any names and so God sent Adam to do the job.

## Lilith

Lilith means nocturnal being. She was a she-devil, a killer of children, and according to one legend, she was the first to seduce Adam. In the frame around the picture are poison-berries because she was evil.

## The Seventh Day

This is the day after God finished his work of creating the world, when he found the result good and blessed it. The corn is a sign that God has given fertility and prosperity so that all creatures and people may eat. The owl, King of the Birds, is a symbol of wisdom. Hovering beside Eve is a suggestion of stories that have been told about the serpent in the Garden of Eden actually being a human being.

## Expelled from Paradise

Adam and Eve on the way out of Paradise, exiled, as we all are, from the Garden of Eden. The serpent is sorry to see Eve go. Adam takes an animal out with him and Eve has some apples to keep in reserve. In Paradise they didn't have to do anything, but now that they are going out into the world they will have to find ways of surviving.

## Adam and Eve Mourning Abel

Here you can see Adam and his wife mourning the death of their son Abel. Eve grieves over his corpse. Behind them is Cain, condemned by God to wandering the earth as a punishment for the murder of his brother. The flames in the background remind us of what caused this terrible thing to happen: Abel, who was a kind, good man, made a sacrifice to God and God welcomed it. But when Cain made *his* sacrifice, God rejected him. This made Cain mad with jealousy and he went out into the fields and killed Abel. He thought he had acted in secret, but the eyes had seen him, God had seen him. He thought he could run away to somewhere where no-one would know what he had done. But he was never to escape.

Adam and Eve were so grief-stricken and shocked. They did not even know what they should do with the body. But a raven flew down carrying the body of one of her young, and scratched at the earth and buried the tiny bird. Then Adam knew what to do with the body of Abel.

Two things in particular made me paint this picture: I wanted to convey the idea of these poor parents having to cope with something that was more awful, more terrible than anything they could possibly have imagined, and secondly, to show that if you do something wrong, you can never escape from it. Cain was haunted by his crime for the rest of his days.

## Cain and Abel

In this picture I have tried to sum up the story of Cain, starting with the sacrifice made by Abel which sparked off the tragedy of Cain's jealous murder of his own brother. God then devised a punishment for this dreadful crime: he condemned Cain to wander through all the countries of the world and made a mark on his forehead indicating that no-one was allowed to kill him.

In the background are symbols of some of the places through which Cain passed: a Buddhist temple, a Catholic church, a gabled roof in Holland, a memorial chapel where the souls of the dead people are prayed for, but of all places this was the one denied to Cain, for there was no rest for his soul, no relief from his pain.

Legend has it that one day Cain was trudging through a wood belonging to a rich man whose favourite pastime was hunting. The man was, however, blind, so he had a servant who told him exactly where to aim. The servant saw a wild animal, instructed his master to fire, but did not notice that Cain was in the bushes behind it, and at that moment Cain was finally killed.

The wheel symbolises Cain's destiny and also that the world has no beginning and no end, and the two lions are the emblem of Israel.

## Joseph in Captivity

After Joseph had been sold to merchants by his treacherous brothers, he was bought as a slave by the captain of the Egyptian guard, Potiphar. Joseph was soon so trusted that he looked after everything for his master. His master's wife quickly saw how handsome their new servant was and tried to interest him in her charms. But Joseph did not react, as he was determined not to displease his master. This angered his master's wife, and she managed to pretend that, far from rejecting her advances, Joseph had tried to seduce her. This of course made Potiphar very angry, and Joseph was flung into prison. There he met two people who had offended the Pharaoh, his cook and his serving boy. These two were very distressed because they had had vivid dreams and there was no one in prison to interpret them. It wasn't long before they realised Joseph was something special, and somehow it got out that he knew how to interpret dreams. So they asked him to do this for them. Joseph told the serving boy, 'You will be acquitted and eventually set free. When this happens, put in a word for me with the Pharaoh because I am innocent.' The baker, however, was to be less lucky. On the left in the picture you can see the baker hanged, with an Egyptian symbol of death, a bird, and then the body packed up in a boat to be cast on to the Nile. His widow sits below and mourns.

The serving boy did indeed survive, but he forgot all about his promise and Joseph spent almost two more years in prison. Then one day, the Pharaoh was deeply troubled by some dreams and one of his staff, the serving boy, remembering the man who had interpreted his dream so accurately in prison, had Joseph brought to the Pharaoh. The upshot of the story was that he was not only released from prison, but also made Minister of Agriculture because of his wise interpretation of the Pharaoh's dream.

## The Hungry Ones

Here are two different sorts of hungry people. At the window are some poor, thin children gazing in at a family who have plenty to eat but, despite their loaded table, they are also hungry, not for food but for happiness.

# Jewish Wedding

A traditional Jewish wedding. The chupah, or canopy, symbolises the home in which this young couple will live. The little boy brings the prayer shawl that the bridegroom will put on after the ceremony.

## Celebration in the Synagogue

## After the Wedding

This is the party after a wedding ceremony. The youngest of three daughters is getting married. The parents are losing their last daughter, but they are nevertheless pleased for her in her happiness. The dancing is beginning and, with the traditional show of modesty, the other daughters hold kerchiefs in their hands lest there should be any fleshly contact between them and their husbands in public. The little girl on the right wants to dance. She doesn't understand the importance of the convention of not touching yet, but the older boy she is asking is more careful.

# An Ancient Synagogue

The barrels outside contain water that the men use to cleanse themselves before they enter the synagogue. The young man has a prayer shawl over his arm and in the corner sits a woman who is not allowed into the synagogue, so she prays outside, listening to what is going on. Inside, the two hands make a symbolic gesture for a special prayer. Above is the eternal flame and high up are the two tablets of truth.

## Moses Triptych 1

The story of Moses is huge and complicated as well as being very important indeed. It fills five books in the Bible. But I have tried to pick out some of the key events in these paintings. At the time when Moses was born, the Pharaoh had tried to limit the population of Jews in Egypt by ordering all boy babies to be killed at birth, but Moses had slipped through the net. He was adopted by the Pharaoh's daughter and brought up in the Egyptian court, but as he grew up he was strongly drawn by a kind of inner affinity to his people, the Jews. One day Moses saw some of them being used as forced labour, pounding clay for bricks. An overseer stood by abusing them. Moses was outraged and killed the man. And so he had to flee from Egypt to escape punishment for his crime. My series of pictures begins at this point. After some days' travelling, Moses, who had no food and no money, found work as a shepherd for the priest of a tribe of nomads. Soon he married one of the priest's daughters. One day, while searching for new pastures, Moses suddenly saw an extraordinary sight: a bush that was full of flames but not actually burning up. Then to his astonishment there came from the burning bush the words, 'Take off your shoes, you are on holy ground,' followed by an instruction from God that Moses must go and persuade the Pharaoh to let him lead his fellow Jews out of slavery in Egypt. At first, Moses was very intimidated at this idea, and said he was no good at speeches, but then God reassured him by giving him certain magical powers that he could use to impress the Pharaoh, and by telling him to get his brother Aaron to do the talking. Moses became preoccupied with the idea of freeing his countrymen and set off for Egypt with his wife and children.

# *Moses Triptych 2*

The second triptych begins with Moses and Aaron in the Egyptian court. They had obtained an audience with the Pharaoh, and asked in the name of God, 'Let my people go.' But of course the Pharaoh refused. Moses realised that they had to make the Pharaoh think that they were something special, and then he might listen to them. So, using his new talents, he started to prove that he was a magician, and changed his staff into a snake. But the Pharaoh was not impressed and produced courtiers who could do the same. Next Aaron made his staff swallow up their staffs. But it became clear that even though Moses and Aaron could outdo the Egyptians, the Jews would remain in slavery. Then, through Moses, God inflicted a series of terrible plagues on the Egyptians. Each time, when things were at their worst, the Pharaoh would say the Jews could leave, but when the situation improved, he went back on his promise. Finally, the worst plague of all happened: the firstborn of every Egyptian family mysteriously died. This time the Pharaoh was desperate, for his own son was dead, and he told the troublemaker to lead his people out of Egypt. Although it was night-time, Moses knew that they must leave immediately, so he gathered the people together and they left in great haste. Every spring, this Exodus is remembered in the Jewish festival of the Passover, and for seven days only unleavened bread is eaten, recalling the hurried departure. So Moses led the Jews out of Egypt and across the desert towards the sea. Meanwhile, the Pharaoh had realised that the Jews, all the slave labour in the country, really were escaping, and he changed his mind and ordered his men to chase after them. Soon the Jews were in real danger and they began to panic. But God told Moses to stretch his staff over the sea to make a path for his people. Moses did this, and, miraculously, the waters parted to the right and the left and the sea bed became dry land. The Egyptians followed in hot pursuit, but immediately they attempted to use the miraculous path, they got bogged down in the mud. Realising that God was not with them, they tried to abandon the chase, but, with his people safely on the other side, Moses waved his hand over the sea again and the water returned to its original position, covering all the Pharaoh's chariots, cavalry and army. Not one Egyptian survived.

The Jews now faced forty years of wandering in the desert and survived by living off manna from heaven and water that Moses made spring from a rock by striking it with his staff. At last they reached Mount Sinai. This was the holy place where Moses had seen the burning bush and he was called up the mountain by God. Suddenly there was a huge noise, thunder claps, lightning and the sound of a loud trumpet. Moses seemed to grow huge and towering. Then God pronounced to Moses the Ten Commandments. You can see in his hands the two tablets of stone that God had instructed him to bring up the sacred mountain. In my picture they carry the initials in Hebrew of the Ten Commandments.

Many years later, from a high point in the mountains, God showed Moses the beautiful sight of the Promised Land and although Moses died before he reached it, his people finally arrived there.

*Moses and the Pharaoh*

*Exodus*

*Moses on Mount Sinai*

## Scenes from Spinoza's Life

Usually I have the background information for my pictures tucked away in the back of my mind, but I only knew a little about Spinoza: that he was a free thinker, and that he had been excommunicated by the Jewish community. I didn't know why. It took Siegfried, my husband, six months to explain the story of Spinoza to me so that it was familiar enough for me to be able to conjure up this picture with many parts. I painted it for the cover of a book on Spinoza edited by my husband. Spinoza's parents lived in Spain at the time of the Inquisition and here you see the results for Jewish people. If they refused to accept Christianity they were burned at the stake. As they had either to accept the cross or perish, some of them pretended to take on the Christian faith, but in reality they still attended Jewish synagogues, which had gone underground. I have included a couple who are desperate as they face the decision of lying to stay alive or staying true and dying. Anyway, Spinoza's parents decided to leave the country, for it was no place to bring up their young son for whom they had high hopes, and they fled to Holland. There Spinoza studied and did very well. He was fascinated with ideas and was a man with a very open, free mind, interested in all aspects of whatever issue or subject he was confronting. When he grew up, he earned his living by grinding optical lenses. But there were certain people in the Jewish community where he lived who disliked Spinoza and what they thought of as his over-liberal views. This dislike grew to hatred as they became more and more convinced that Spinoza was an heretic who should not be tolerated within the community. One night Spinoza dreamt that a tall black man had come to his bedside and passed his hand over Spinoza's eyes. This he took to be a sign that his death was near. The two rabbis in the pictures on his wall were people who were away from Amsterdam when he was being chased out. Had they been there, they would have prevented the witch hunt against him. The next day the leaders of the campaign against Spinoza came to his house, excommunicated him from the faith, cast him out of his home, far away from the people he knew, saying that he was not fit to stay with them. Isolated and excluded, Spinoza was now a sad man and it was not long before he died. His body was buried in a grave in a churchyard without a proper stone by his grieving sister.

## Job and his Friends

Job was a prosperous and righteous man who had always been obedient to God. One day the Devil came to God and said, 'Why do you give this man so much? He has a lovely wife, he has children and more riches than anyone else. Why do you favour him so?' 'Because he is obedient,' answered God. 'He believes in me and he loves me.' Then the Devil said, 'If you were to take all that he owns away from him, then you would see whether he really loved you.' God thought about this and it did seem like a real test. So he took all Job's riches away from him, and one night, while Job's children were dining at the home of his eldest son, a whirlwind struck the house and they were all killed. But Job still remained firm in his faith, and would only say, 'The Lord gives and the Lord takes away, blessed be the Lord.' So then the Devil made another suggestion, 'The only true test now is to deny him his health.' Immediately Job fell ill and became covered in sores. My picture shows him trying to relieve some of the terrible itching with a comb. Three of his friends, having heard about Job's misfortunes, have come to visit him and are shocked at the change that has come over him.

Eventually there was a happy ending to this dreadful story. When Job's submission to God was shown without doubt to be complete and utterly unshakeable, God restored to him double everything he had had before; he had a new family and went on to live to a very great age.

## Balaam's Wonder Ass

Balaam was a famous wise man and magician. King Balak wanted Balaam's help in getting rid of a large number of Israelites who, on their way to the Promised Land, had pitched camp in his kingdom. But Balaam, who knew that God regarded the Israelites as his people, replied that he could not help. Then the king sent three of his ministers to offer Balaam a huge reward for his services and to tell him that he must come. This time Balaam reluctantly went with them. Suddenly, on the way up a hill Balaam's donkey stopped stock still and refused to move a step further. Balaam beat her to try to make her carry on, but it made no difference because she could see what none of the others had seen: an angel blocking the path ahead. When Balaam continued to beat her, she spoke to him, asking why he hurt her so when he loved her and she was serving him just as she always had. Then Balaam saw the angel and promised there and then that he would say only what God wanted. So when he was taken to a place high above the encampment, he made sacrifices and, to King Balak's anger, blessed the people of Israel, rather than damning them as the king had wanted. But Balaam was such a powerful soothsayer that King Balak could do nothing but send him home.

# The Boy and his Donkey

This is a little story from the country. The boy was tired of staying at home with his mother. He wanted to go and explore over the mountains and across the sea. But when he told his mother of his plans, she said he was too young to go wandering off on his own. So he went along to the stable and led out the donkey, and then started off on his adventure with his friend. I have always liked donkeys – I often put them into my pictures.

*Ploughing*

## The Noonday Witch

This represents a story I know from Prague. One day a few years ago I was listening to the radio and I heard a piece of music by Dvořák being announced called The Noonday Witch. It was based on the same story and prompted me to paint this picture. The family lives in one room: the kitchen, sitting-room and bedroom are all in the same room. The little boy has been naughty and his mother, who is tired, gets angry with him and says that if he is not good the noonday witch will come and carry him away. He goes on whining and moping and sure enough the witch comes to get him. But all of a sudden the boy's father arrives home from fetching water and the witch rushes to escape through the window, knocking over a flower-pot in her haste. A friend in Czechoslovakia told me that, even now, some old people don't like children to go out at midday for fear of the noonday witch.

## The Dying Mother

The little girl doesn't understand just how ill her mother is, and brings her her slippers, expecting her to get up. I once saw a little girl shaking her mother's shoulder but her mother was dead like a stone. The faithful family dog stays close by, knowing something is wrong.

## The Living Scarecrow

It is night-time. A man is so poor, has been out of work for so long and is so desperate that he decides that the only possibility is to work as a scarecrow. His eyes are red with tiredness and worry, and his children and their friends don't really understand why he is standing there making his arms turn around like the sails of a windmill. But there in the sky are the friendly spirits of the night, keeping watch over him.

## The Dispossessed

## Kol Nidre: The Eve of Atonement

It is evening. The family have finished the last food they will eat until sunset the following day. For tomorrow is Yom Kippur, when they will fast, atone for all their wrongdoings and say prayers of penitence. Before they go to the synagogue the mother prays and blesses the candles.

# Mother Rachel

In some prayers, Mother Rachel is referred to as the Holy Mother of Israel. There is a shrine to her up in the hills above Jerusalem, and when people are worried or troubled in any way, they go up there and pray to Mother Rachel for comfort and help. Here are some of these people – including someone being persecuted by an Egyptian – and the vision of Mother Rachel that some of them get while praying. Her tomb is at a holy place near where Mary, mother of Jesus, is buried.

# *The Flight to Egypt*

This is a beautiful subject, one that is very important to me – the idea of a mother fleeing from danger with her child. A mother, especially of a very young child, feels different from other people. The earthquake in Mexico recently reminded me of this feeling of the wonder of small, new life – the little babies who were pulled from the rubble alive after so many days was an extraordinary, miraculous phenomenon. It seemed that there was something so mighty that it could save these babies from what looked like certain death. There is a parallel for me with the dangers we are going through now: my feeling is that Mary and her child will be saved, just as I believe we will be. The candles lit along the way symbolise her safe journey, and angels watch over her. This image is separate from any idea that the baby would be Christ and that there would be differences between Jews and Christians later, for I find these divisions very sad.

## The Life of Christ

Here I have tried to include as many scenes from the life of Christ as possible on one canvas. At the Last Supper, Jesus knew that shortly he would be hunted down and that in his hour of need most of his friends would desert him. On the cross is a lamb being sacrificed, signifying the innocence of Jesus. His claim to be King of the Jews was not meant in the way that his enemies thought. On the right are the money lenders whom he chased out of the temple. The lady leaning back against the houses on the left is looking on with great despair. She has not got involved in all this political business but she knows that a terrible injustice has been done. Candles are burned in the Jewish tradition to mark mourning or celebration – here the crucifixion and the resurrection.

# Mary's Vision After the Crucifixion

Jesus had a premonition that he would not live until the evening of the Feast of the Passover, Seder. Very early on Friday morning he was picked up by Roman soldiers and condemned to be crucified – this was the equivalent of, say, being shot by military police nowadays. In the Jewish tradition it is very important for all celebrations to be properly observed, especially so that the children understand that the Passover, for instance, reminds us that the Jews were saved from the final plague in Egypt. But can you imagine how hard it was for a mother whose son had been crucified at midday to have a Passover celebration in the evening? Before evening his body had been taken down from the cross because in Jewish law it is a dishonour for a person's corpse to remain unburied over a Friday night. In her grief, Mary imagines that her dead son has come along. Kind neighbours help with the jobs she would usually do herself. It is an old custom that after the last cups of wine have been drunk and blessed, one cup is put on the table for the prophet Elijah and not touched by anyone. The door is left open and he enters and drinks and consoles the sad and the bereaved.

## The Little Red Shoe

When the Germans occupied Rumania, they took a lot of people from Czernowitz, over the Dniester river to work camps in Transnistria. A lot of people died and a lot of people were shot. When the Russians defeated the Germans, they brought back the people who were left and among them were children. When they got to Czernowitz they took all the children who had no relatives to the marketplace and asked for people to adopt them. I remember one rabbi, such a thin, delicate man that you would think he scarcely had the energy to live. But he collected over forty children and took them back to the single room where he lived with his wife and son, and looked after them. When the beautiful little girl in this picture arrived back in Czernowitz, all she brought with her was one tiny little red shoe, that she kept with her all the time. When we asked her why she would not let go of it, she told us this story: when she was being marched along the long road by soldiers she was carrying her little baby brother. But he cried a lot, as babies do, and finally a soldier lost patience and killed it and threw it away. All the little girl could salvage was one little shoe. She took it with her, like a talisman. I painted this picture many, many years after I heard the story. But for me it was a sort of laying to rest of a sad image, a painful memory.

## Vision of a Gas Chamber

This was one of the first pictures I painted. It is not a scene I actually saw, but one that stayed in mind from the stories I heard after the war. The women have been told to take their clothes off so that they can go for a shower, but in fact they are being herded into the gas chamber. Outside are people protesting to no avail, and death stalks those who are left.

## Tereczin

Some years after the war, I visited Prague and went to the Jewish museum, which had an exhibition of paintings by children who had been in the concentration camp at Tereczin. They had become orphans when their parents were taken away. Whenever the authorities knew that the Red Cross was making a visit, they would clean the place up and give better food rations to the children. But at least the Red Cross sent paper and pencils and things to do. Among the pictures were bright, happy scenes of things the children remembered from their home lives – they seem to have been more able than the adults to ignore the horrors going on around them, even though death hovered all around. My visits to this small exhibition in the old Ghetto were quite a shattering experience, and I have tried to put my impressions together in this painting, which now hangs in the Holocaust Museum, Jerusalem.

*Butterflies*

## Courting Donkeys

When we first arrived in Israel, Jerusalem still didn't belong only to Israel, and the new arrivals had to be accommodated where there was space. We were in a rather down-at-heel hotel with iron shutters over the windows because of the danger of gunfire, and it was very hot inside and claustrophobic. One day we just couldn't stand the shut-in feeling any more and so, despite the risks, we opened the shutters. Opposite the hotel was an old overgrown garden, still very beautiful, around the ruins of King Solomon's baths, and there, suddenly, my husband and I saw two donkeys dancing for joy like human beings. We hadn't smiled for days or weeks, but this extraordinary, lovely sight made us burst out laughing.

# Negev

Here are two of a series of six paintings I did after visiting Negev. The heat and dryness in these mountains, this desert, were intense, suffocating even, and the few animals we came across were so thin you could see their bones through the skin. But the light was extraordinary, like something that didn't really belong to this world. In the twinkling of an eye the colours changed completely. It was like a *fata morgana*. I wasn't able to paint while I was there, but when I got home and sat in front of the easel, just thinking about the place made the colours jump about in my mind.

# Judah and Tamar

This story is very special to me. Judah was a rich and important man in his community. He had three sons, quite a big household and a lot of animals and fields. He was also very clever and knowledgeable, and if people needed something they came to him to ask for advice. One day a beautiful young woman who was not Jewish but came from a noble family said that she would like to marry his eldest son. Judah agreed and they married. But the couple hadn't been together long and they had had no children when he suddenly died. Tamar was very upset at his death, but in Jewish law, if a husband dies leaving unmarried brothers, a widow has the right to ask for another brother. So then she asked Judah for the second son. Judah knew the Jewish law well, so he realised Tamar was right, and although he was not very happy about her marrying his second son, he agreed. The second son was not at all pleased with the idea, because he believed that Tamar was a woman who would always outlive her husband and he feared for his life. But he married her, and not long after he died. There was a third son who was very young. The father did not want to give him to Tamar. So she became angry and made a plan. In Jerusalem, there was a wall which was the red light district of the city. Tamar knew that Judah would come past this place on his way back from the fields, and she sat on the wall, with a veil over her face, well covered up so that no one would see who she was. When he arrived, she beckoned to him, and asked him to go with her. 'You are very beautiful,' he said, 'but I cannot go with you because I have no money.' 'No matter,' she said, 'as long as you leave me something that belongs to you, and in the morning you can send a servant to pay me and I will return whatever it is you have given me.' Judah agreed, and asked her what she would like to keep in lieu of payment. She asked for his ring, his belt and his stick. He agreed and went with her. In the morning, his servant came to pay her and retrieve his master's belongings. But there was no sign of the mysterious woman, and no one knew anything about her or where she had gone. Time passed. Tamar went on living in the women's section of Judah's house. But then the news got out that she was pregnant. It was a very great sin for a widow to get pregnant, and for such a terrible deed, it was decided that she must be punished according to the law. Judah, as a pillar of the community, was to be the one to judge her and he ordered that she should be stoned to death for her crime. But just as the first stones were being raised, Tamar threw up her veil and revealed the ring, the stick and the belt. Judah inspected them and admitted that they were his and that Tamar was more in the right than him because he had denied her his third son, and so she was saved.

# The Witch of Endor

Israel was at war with the Philistines. Saul, King of Israel, was very worried at the size and strength of the enemy's army and waited for a sign from God, in a dream or a prophecy, to tell him what to do. But he received no such help. Usually Saul would have consulted a wise old prophet called Samuel, but he had recently died. Now he had a difficulty, for the next best thing was to get a witch to conjure up the spirit of Samuel, but Saul had in the past been very intolerant of witches, believing them to have too much influence, and most of them had been banished or executed. So now he went in disguise to the famous witch of Endor, and asked her to call up the spirit of Samuel. 'What a terrible thing to ask,' she said, 'Saul will have me killed.' But her visitor promised that she would be safe. It is said that when the witch called up the spirits of ordinary people, they came to her upside down, but when she summoned up special spirits they appeared head upwards. Seeing the ghostly figure of Samuel the right way up, she put two and two together and realised that it was Saul himself who was with her, and she shrieked 'Did you come here to have me killed?' But Saul reassured her. He was much more anxious to communicate with the spirit of the dead prophet. The king could not see the spirit, but he heard Samuel's voice, which said 'Why have you disturbed me and conjured me up like this?' Saul replied that he needed urgently to know what was going to happen to him in the war. Then the voice of the prophet said, 'Why do you ask me this? I foretold years ago that because you had not done what God asked you to do, you would lose not only your kingdom, but also your life. And that is what will happen.' The king went on to fight and suffered a terrible wound, so bad that he decided to finish the job and fell on his own sword. On the right of the picture you can see the symbolic act of a servant taking the king's mantle to David who was to be the next King of Israel.

## Argyle Cut

This was one of the first paintings I made in Australia of somewhere I believe has now disappeared. It was a place near the harbour in Sydney opposite where the opera house now is.

## Australian Waratah Tree

## Australian Aborigines

This shows the life of the Aborigines in the desert. There are caves with cave paintings where their ancestors used to live, and all this is in the Red Mountains – a mysterious place where people disappear and are never found. It is so hot, so dry. The animals die. The trees have no leaves. The flowers towards the back of the picture are my attempt to express the different aspects of the people: their simple charm, their suffering and their anger about the suffering. That is why there are teeth among the flowers. I felt for these people who had suffered such abuse.

## Lady in the Bath

A fantasy picture. The shadowy head is a suggestion of someone the lady is thinking about, whom she might wish was in the bath with her.

*Australian Lagoon*

## Barrier Reef

Just once, when we lived in Australia, we went to the Great Barrier Reef and took a trip in a glass-bottomed boat, and the sight through the bottom of the boat was one of the most beautiful I have ever seen. In the jewel-like blue water were fantastic corals of exquisite colours, and all sorts of strange and wonderful fish, and sea-creatures with tails like flowers.

# The Blue Adria

Children have come to this fairy-tale spot to spend their Sunday afternoon. The place is so beautiful that they are content to sit on the bench and gaze out to sea, towards the castle in the distance. Actually the castle is a fortress in Yugoslavia that for many years protected the country from its enemies and was never taken.

*In the Steppes of Central Asia: Homage to Borodin*

## Night on the Bare Mountain: Homage to Mussorgsky

Here are the witches, who are powerful only in the dark, and must flee the light. The cock is starting to crow, the church bell is ringing and they realise that day is about to begin.

## The Gipsy Girl

The gipsies I knew about when I lived in Europe never married. Perhaps this gipsy girl has been abandoned by the father of her children. There are empty bottles from his drinking, his tools have all been left where they fell, even his fiddle lies forgotten. So the gipsy girl faces a lonely life, forever camping on the outskirts of villages or towns, and now she must look after her children on her own.

## The Crystal Ball

This shows jobless people trying to find out about their future. Being jobless is bitter and poisonous like the serpents. But the angel, representing hope, is peaceful and reassuring, telling the people that although there will be some evil, good will triumph in the end.

## On the Other Side of the Fence

# The Women's Concert

It always seems to me that it is men who play in concerts, so here is a concert with only women.

*Joyful Street Life*

## After the Storm

There are some very dangerous and stormy waters off Australia and even the most experienced fishermen cannot be certain they will return when they go out to sea. Here are the womenfolk looking out for their husbands, but not all of them will come back.

*Homage to Grandma Moses*

## The Bespoke Overcoat

This is a very sad tale similar to one written by Gogol, and made into a film by Wolf Mankowitz. It concerns a thin, poverty-stricken accountant and his friend, a tailor. The accountant worked in a clothing factory but couldn't afford to buy himself one of the good, warm overcoats he saw being made there. He and his friend the tailor both got drunk one night and hatched a plan to steal a coat, but the plan went wrong and the poor, deprived accountant still had no protection from the bitter winter. So the tailor promised to make him a coat. But he was an idle man, and he never got around to finishing it. The next thing he knew his friend the accountant was dead. The tailor was so distressed. He took the half-finished coat and threw it into the grave with the corpse. My picture shows the tailor in his room after the burial, when he has lit a candle and said a prayer for the soul of his dead friend. Suddenly the vision of the corpse comes back to haunt him, bringing back the coat which arrived too late to be any use.

## Erlking 1

There is a poem by Goethe that tells of a sick child being carried through the night by his father. The child has a high fever: he is convinced that there are ghosts in the wood and he is terrified, especially of the King of the Spirits, who whispers to him, 'Come with me to the Rhine, where there are maidens to play and dance and sing with you.' The boy pleads with his father not to let the Erlking get him. The father, who cannot see or hear what is going on, comforts his child, telling him that there is nothing to be frightened of – it is only the wind rustling in the branches. But the little boy is convinced he is going to be spirited away.

## Erlking 2

When, after a long and difficult journey, the riders finally reach their destination, the little boy is dead in his father's arms.

# The Cabbalist

Cabbala is an ancient Jewish mystical tradition. A man must be of mature mind, at least over thirty years old, before he embarks on its study.

# *Merkaba*

Merkaba is Hebrew for a cart or a chariot. This picture shows the Vision of Ezekiel. He saw a horseless chariot with four wheels, one inside the other, and every wheel had eyes on it. Around this curious sight were four beings – one had a human form with angel wings, one was a lion, also with wings, one was an eagle and one an ox. On the ground, face down because he is so frightened by his vision, is Ezekiel. But he can feel the hand of God resting on his head, comforting him. The chariot is transported to heaven by flames, and the angels keep watch. The fish in the water is a symbol of celebration; in the Jewish faith fish is eaten on the eve of a holiday, before Yom Kippur, before the New Year, before the celebration of the Torah being given to Moses, even on a Friday night, the eve of the Sabbath.

## Daniel's Vision

Daniel was a special person who was entrusted by God with visions. One day he was with three friends on the banks of a river when suddenly a curious-looking man clothed in linen appeared, hovering above the water nearby. The others saw nothing but a great fear came upon them and they crept away. Daniel was overcome and when he heard the vision speaking, he collapsed on the ground in a trance. But then he felt a consoling hand on him, helping him up, and a voice comforted him saying, 'Don't be afraid. The reason I have come to you is that you are especially chosen by God.'

## Daniel in the Lions' Den

Daniel was a favourite of King Darius. He had shown great ability and soon the king planned to make him chief administrator of the kingdom. But the other ministers in the court became jealous of Daniel. They persuaded the king to make a decree that anyone found worshipping a god or man other than the king should be thrown into the lions' den. Daniel, as usual, prayed to God three times a day, and the ministers reported this to the king. Then King Darius was in a difficult position, for there was no doubt that the decree had been broken, and the ministers said, 'Why do you treat this boy as something special? He is just an ordinary disobedient man, not a prophet. Just try putting him in with the lions and you will see how special he is.' At first the king resisted, but in the end he reluctantly agreed to put Daniel in the lions' den. The king fasted and could not sleep. Early the next morning, he sent a message to where Daniel had been taken and soon the messenger came to the king with news of an extraordinary sight. Daniel, who had put his faith in God, was sitting quite peacefully among the lions, reading. Then all the ministers who had caused such trouble were thrown to the lions, which were by now very hungry, and Darius decreed that throughout his kingdom the God of Daniel should be worshipped.

## Elijah and Elisha

Elisha was a simple shepherd who greatly admired the power of his master, the prophet Elijah, to do good and to stand up for what was right. When Elijah realised that God was going to take him away, he asked whether Elisha had any requests to make of his master. Elisha replied, 'I would like your strength' Elijah explained that it was very difficult to pass this on, but that if Elisha was able to see Elijah at the moment God took him away, then he would be able to take on Elijah's mantle and receive his powers. If Elisha saw nothing, then he would get nothing. Here is Elisha throwing away his shepherd's crook and bidding farewell to his parents, for he has indeed seen Elijah being carried up high into the sky in a chariot pulled by horses of fire, and the mantle has been cast down to him.

## Noah's Ark

All the naked people in the middle of this picture show why this disaster happened. The people were very loose and had been very wicked, so God made a flood. Noah was the only good man left, so God instructed him to build an ark and escape the flood with his family and two of every living creature. On the left is Noah with his ark and his two sons helping him. The water is rising all the time and his sons are frightened that they will be engulfed: 'What are you waiting

for?' they ask. But Noah is still confident that the few creatures which are missing will turn up. On the right, the ark and its passengers have arrived at their destination. Noah is not a tee-totaller and he has some wine with him to celebrate their arrival. With him are his three sons and daughters-in-law and his wife; the dove that brought the message to him from God is sitting on his shoulder.

## King Solomon and The Queen of Sheba

The Queen of Sheba had heard of King Solomon's fame, so she went to visit him with a huge and fabulous entourage. Solomon fell in love with this woman who was not just rich and beautiful, but also extremely intelligent, and gave her everything she wanted.

## David and Bathsheba

The day was drawing to a close, but it was still hot, so Bathsheba could bathe outside. Her home was in part of King David's palace, and, unbeknown to her, the love-sick king was watching her. He was so attracted by her beauty that he asked her to come to him, and she did. Soon it was clear that Bathsheba was pregnant, but there was a problem: she was already married. So King David used his power to arrange for her husband, a soldier, to come back from the war so that the child would seem to be his, and then straight away after fixed for him to be sent where the fighting was very fierce. It was not long before Bathsheba's husband was killed, and soon King David married Bathsheba. He had got his own way, but God was greatly displeased.

## House on the Waterfall

A fantasy picture. The woman lives alone and spins. Perhaps some terrible tragedy or disappointment has befallen her. There is no path, no contact with other people, the animals are her only company, and she lives her solitary life with the constant noise of the waterfall. She is a sad person but has a kind of serenity in her beautiful, isolated retreat.

## Midnight Dancers

There is a place in Austria, high in the hills above Salzburg, that I visited when I was taking a cure at a spa in the area. When Jimmy Carter was President of the United States, he attended a conference there with President Sadat of Egypt to try to make peace for Israel. It is supposed to be one of the most beautiful places in the world with meadows sweeping down to a lake. Here I have painted a hot summer night, when people have gone up there to enjoy themselves. As always at a dance, there is somebody left alone. The children of the young mother are tired and fretful and want to leave, but maybe she is waiting for someone to dance with. The angel watches fondly over the whole scene and a cherub joins in the swimming. I painted in three moons so that they could all have a bit more light.

## Speakers' Corner

Speakers' Corner represents something I admire very much in Britain and had heard about when I lived in Australia. Everybody is entitled to speak out. So I have painted all the races together. The Jew and the Arab stand together at the front because, you see, however much they want to deny it, they did originally come from the same race. I am not interested in politics. All the races are mixed up now so there is no point in trying to emphasise their separateness. That only leads to conflict. There is a Frenchman who has settled in London and a typical English-man striding through the crowd not looking to the right or left. A policeman looks on benignly. The man with the red flag shouts about freedom and peace, but he is the angriest one there.

# Under Milk Wood

I could paint picture after picture of the life that Dylan Thomas described in *Under Milk Wood*. Here is the little town waking up: the children are going to school, the shops are opening, blind old Captain Cat sits in his house listening to the world go by . . . What really inspired me to paint this was the preacher's prayer, which for some reason touches me very deeply:

Every morning when I wake,
Dear Lord, a little prayer I make,
O please to keep Thy lovely eye
On all poor creatures born to die.

And every evening at sun-down
I ask a blessing on the town,
For whether we last the night or no
I'm sure is always touch-and-go.

We are not wholly bad or good
Who live our lives under Milk Wood,
And Thou, I know, wilt be the first
To see our best side, not our worst.

O let us see another day!
Bless us this holy night, I pray,
And to the sun we all will bow
And say, good-bye – but just for now!

# EXHIBITIONS

## Solo Shows

| | |
|---|---|
| 1963 | Rudy Komon Gallery, Sydney |
| 1966 | White Studio Exhibition Gallery, Beaumont, Adelaide |
| 1968 | Brian Johnstone Gallery, Brisbane |
| 1970 | Kim Bonython Gallery, Sydney |
| 1974 | Portal Gallery, London |
| 1979 | Barry Stern Galleries, Sydney |
| 1980 | Hamilton Gallery, London |
| 1983 | Galeria Contini, Caracas |

## Mixed Shows

1964: Blake Society, Sydney; Von Bertouch Galleries, Newcastle, New South Wales; Contemporary Art Society of NSW, David Jones Art Gallery, Sydney, and Farmer's Blaxland Gallery, Sydney. 1965: Gallery 'A', Sydney; Dominion Art Gallery, Sydney; Contemporary Art Society of NSW, Dominion Art Gallery, Sydney; Blake Society, Sydney; Gallery 'A', Melbourne, Sydney and Canberra; Von Bertouch Galleries, Newcastle, New South Wales. 1966: Blake Society, Sydney; Macquarie Galleries, Canberra; Von Bertouch Galleries, Newcastle, New South Wales; Christmas Art Exhibition, Farmer's Blaxland Gallery, Sydney; Contemporary Art Society, NSW, Dominion Art Gallery, Sydney; Gallery 'A', Sydney. 1967: Gallery 'A', Sydney and Melbourne; Flotta Laura Art Prizes, Sydney; Christmas Exhibition, Farmer's Blaxland Gallery, Sydney; Mosman Gallery, Sydney; Blake Society, Sydney; Woollahra Municipal Council, Sydney. 1968: 'Art Affair' at Whitehall Hotel, Rushcutters Bay, Sydney; Arts Vietnam, Gallery 'A', Sydney; Blake Society, Sydney; The Gallery Australis, Sydney; Christmas Exhibition, Farmer's Blaxland Gallery, Sydney; Macquarie Galleries, Canberra. 1969: Blake Society, Sydney; Contemporary Art Society NSW, Gallery 'A', Sydney; Moomba Festival, Toorak Gallery, Melbourne; National Gallery of Victoria, Carnegie Collection. 1970: Moomba Art Festival, Toorak Gallery, Melbourne; Blake Society, Sydney. 1970/71: Great Synagogue, Sydney. 1971: Macquarie Galleries, Canberra; Blake Society, Sydney. 1975: Commonwealth Institute, London; New Zealand House, London; Musée Henri Rousseau, Laval, France. 1976: Whiterock House Gallery, Bakewell, Derbyshire. 1977: Australia Galleries, Melbourne. 1978: Summer Exhibition, Hammersmith Town Hall, London; Portal Gallery, London; Musée de l'Ile de France, Vicq, France; Eisenmann Galerie, Böblingen, Germany. 1979: Kasper Galerie, Morges, Geneva; Portal Gallery, London; Eisenmann Galerie, Böblingen, Germany; First International of Naives, Hamilton Gallery, London. 1980: Australian Artists, New South Wales House, London; Eisenmann Galerie, Böblingen, Germany; Portal Gallery, London. 1981: Collection of Musée de l'Ile de France, Vicq, Ville de Paris; Eisenmann Galerie, Böblingen, Germany; Portal Gallery, London. 1982: Musée International d'Art Naïf Anatole Jakovsky, Nice. 1983: Museum of Contemporary Art, Chicago; Eisenmann Galerie, Böblingen, Germany. 1984: Festival of Arts, Bath; Portal Gallery, London. 1985: Ben Uri Gallery, London; Australian Galleries, Melbourne; Municipal Theatre Gallery, Brive, France. 1986: Galeria Contini, Caracas, Venezuela; Galerie Neumühle, Schlangenbad/Wiesbaden, Germany; Portal Gallery, London.

# SELECTED BIBLIOGRAPHY

S. Blanchard *La Chanson Traditionelle et les Naïfs* Editions Max Fourny, Paris, 1975

O. Bihalji-Merin and Nebojša-Bato Tomašević *World Encyclopedia of Naive Art* Frederick Muller, London, 1984

Pearl Binder *Magic Symbols of the World* Hamlyn, London, 1972

P. Camby *Le Paradis et les Naïfs* Editions Max Fourny, Paris, 1983

D. Craig *Australian Art Auctions Records* Sydney, 1975

M. Fourny *Album Mondial de la Peinture Naive* Editions Hervas, Paris, 1981

M. Germain *Artists and Galleries of Australia* Sydney, 1979 and 1984

P. Hessing 'On My Primitive Painting', *Leonardo* vol. 9 no. 12, Paris, 1977.

P. Hessing 'Painting, An Occupation of One in Old Age', *Leonardo* vol. 12 no. 4, Paris, 1979.

S. Hessing *Speculum Spinozanum* Routledge & Kegan Paul, London/Boston, 1977

A. Jakovsky *Lexicon of Naive Painters*, second edition, Basilius Verlag, Basel, 1976

E. Lister *Portal Painters* Alpine Publishers, New York, 1981.

B. McCullough *Australian Naive Painters* Hill of Content Publishers, Melbourne, 1977

Museum of Contemporary Art, Chicago *Naive and Outsider Painting from Germany* (catalogue), 1983

J. Olsen *Naive Painters in Art and Australia* Sydney, 1964

L. Pauwels *L'Arche de Noë et les Naïfs* Editions Max Fourny, Paris, 1977

W. Rushton *Adam and Eve*, Bell & Hyman, London, 1985

Philip Vann 'Three Immigrant Naive Painters in Search of Their Roots', *The Artist* vol. 100 no. 3, March 1985

S. Williams and E. Lister *20th Century British Naive Painters* Astragal Books, London, 1977

S. Williams *RONA Guide to Naive Art* London, 1977

S. Williams 'Naives, Primitives and Fantasists', *London Magazine* vol. 17 no. 4, London, October 1977

S. Williams 'Correspondenze', *L'Arte Naive* no. 5, Editrice Age, Reggio Emilia, March 1975